Emergency
Aid
in Schools

First published in Great Britain in 1984 by
The Order of St. John, Priory House,
St. John's Lane, London EC1M 4DA
071–251 2482

2nd edition October 1988 752/48351
3rd edition September 1990 93/54712
2nd impression October 1991 93/58623
4th edition November 1992 123/61096
2nd impression May 1993 1052/62800

ISBN No. 0 900700 40 8

St. John Supplies Product R00034

Designed and printed in England by Lamport Gilbert Limited, Reading

Foreword

From: Robert Balchin MEd., FCP
Chairman
St. John Ambulance National Schools Committee

1 Grosvenor Crescent
London SW1X 7EF

Dear Colleague,

Just occasionally comes the moment dreaded by all of us who look after young people: instead of the usual minor grazes and bruises, we are faced with a severe accident. A child might be drowning or might be bleeding profusely, a staff member could have suffered a heart attack, and *we* have to cope. It is a fearful responsibility and yet there are a few simple procedures that anyone can learn and which, if applied correctly during the first minutes after an accident, could mean the difference between life and death.

These procedures, called Emergency Aid, are detailed in this book with examples of accidents that have actually happened in schools. Over the page is a preface entitled 'How to use this book' and I recommend that you study it carefully before you begin your reading of the main text.

Do remember, however, that, although this little book will equip you with some of the skills that could enable you to deal with a serious accident, it is no substitute for a *course* in First Aid: such a course need not take more than a few hours and details can be found on page 68.

Please keep this book where you can refer to it easily and re-read it regularly, you never know, one of your pupils might have cause to thank you for it someday!

Yours very sincerely,

Robert Balchin

How to use this book

This book has been carefully structured to enable you to use it in three ways:

1. As a form of basic instruction about Emergency Aid;
2. As an aide-mémoire; for 'refresher training';
3. As a reference book in an emergency.

Each of those uses makes certain demands on you as the reader:

Number 1 requires you to read carefully throughout the book taking time to pause and answer the questions within the text, carefully studying the answers when you have done so.

Number 2 requires you to read the book regularly (perhaps once each term).

Number 3 requires you to be familiar with the Emergency Index on page 80 and to keep the book in a handy place.

It is hoped that having read the book you will be willing to undergo further training; details of the courses run by St. John Ambulance are on page 68.

Contents

Action

Let us start by stating an emergency procedure for any situation:

Assess

Make safe

Give Emergency Aid

Inform

You should carry out all those stages at any accident . . . but do not *waste* time.

*Assess the situation, find out what happened and who is injured.

*Make sure that no one else is going to be hurt. (Will *you* be in danger if you go to help? Are on-lookers in danger? Is the casualty in further danger?)

*Give the right Emergency Aid. (So you must read the rest of this book and preferably get further training!)

*Get qualified help and then report the accident using your school's normal procedure.

The first two stages sound fairly straightforward – but are they? Over the next few pages we will look at emergencies which might occur in or around a school and will concentrate on assessing the situation and making it safe.

Here is a fairly typical playground scene:

A child runs up to you and asks for help. She takes you to where a small boy has fallen over and grazed a knee – there is no real emergency, the assessment is obvious and there is nothing that needs making safe. The grazed knee should be cleaned and dressed.

Let us move on to a more serious accident.

You are a science teacher, the class is carrying out an experiment when suddenly you hear breaking glass and a child screams:

What is your assessment and what would you do to make the situation safe?

Assess
The girl has probably got acid on her hand.

Make safe
To make the situation safe you must:

1. Wash that acid off the girl *quickly*.

2. Remove her contaminated clothing.

3. Make certain that no one else is going to be affected.

The general rule to follow is *move the danger, not the casualty.*

Here is another emergency, this time it is morning and you have just arrived at school. You hear a crash behind you, you turn and see that a boy has fallen off his bicycle. This drawing shows the scene:

How would you assess the situation and make it safe?

Assess
The boy seems to have hurt his arm, from the strange angle it is probably broken.

Make safe
You obviously have to get the bicycle off him – and what about his friends? . . . That road looks fairly busy and there could be another accident – so you should ask the crossing attendant to stop all traffic. Also, those other children are going to crowd around and may get in the way. So, unless one of them is a First Aider (and is thus qualified) send them to get help.

You might be tempted to take the boy into the school and wait for an ambulance. Do not do so, it is essential that you *do not move a casualty unless life is at risk.* In this case, moving that arm might make a sharp, broken bone cause a much more serious injury, like damage to a nerve.

Remember, this book will teach you how to deal with an emergency – in many cases (once you have assessed the situation and made it safe) the best thing to do will be nothing except get help and ensure that the casualty's condition does not worsen.

Let us move on and look at the Emergency Aid you should be able to give and when you should provide it.

Breathing

The most serious situation you could be faced with would be seeing a person who would die unless you knew what to do.

Over the next few pages you will be shown some techniques which would save you from having to stand helplessly by as a child or colleague died.

The procedures are simple and straightforward so you should always "have a go" . . . but to be confident that you would be able to carry them out correctly you need to practise.

That practice must only be carried out under qualified supervision (and never on a real person). *

---

*See page 68 for details of courses which provide practice in these techniques.

Let us look at the facts behind the techniques.

*Every cell in the body needs oxygen.

*That oxygen enters the body through the nose and mouth.

*Goes down the windpipe and enters the lungs.

*In the lungs oxygen enters the blood.

*Which is pumped around the body by the heart.

*The oxygen is used by the cells which produce carbon dioxide as waste which the blood carries to the lungs where it is breathed out.

*This whole process of breathing in and out is controlled by a special part of the brain.

A person could die if any of the above stages go wrong.

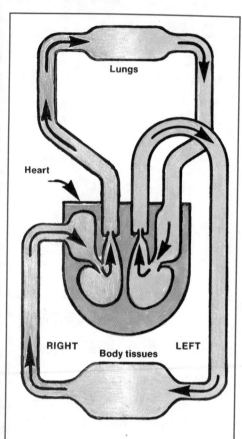

Lungs

Heart

RIGHT **Body tissues** **LEFT**

Potential causes of death are:

Insufficient oxygen (for example in a smoke-filled room).

The nose, mouth or windpipe (airway) is blocked.

The blood is chemically poisoned so that it cannot carry the oxygen.

The heart is not working.

The lungs are not working because the chest is trapped or damaged.

The brain or nerves being damaged so that breathing cannot occur.

ANY OF THESE COULD OCCUR IN A SCHOOL SITUATION

Another point to remember is **that you have 3 minutes to start getting oxygen to the person's brain.** If you do not know what to do, or take more than 3 minutes, then cells in the brain will start to die and the person will have brain damage or will die. On the other hand, if the heart has stopped beating is is essential that an ambulance comes quickly, so dialling 999 is top priority, even if you are on you own.

Summary

To summarize the facts:

Assess the situation and make it safe.
Clear the airway.
Check breathing.
Check pulse.

Act on your findings. If there is a pulse but no breathing, you only need to blow air into the lungs.

If there is no pulse, do not waste time trying to start it unless you know an ambulance has been sent for. Then combine blowing in air with pressing down over the heart to circulate the blood and carry oxygen around the body.

You can check for breathing by looking for movement of the chest and upper abdomen, or listening and feeling for air at the mouth and nose.

You check the pulse in the hollow between the voice box and the main muscle of the neck.

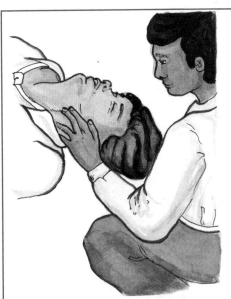

Feel for a pulse in the neck (carotid artery) with your finger-tips, gently pressing the artery against the underlying muscle and bone.

Try it for yourself, you should find that your heart is beating about 72 times per minute (this is an average figure and your rate might be anything between about 60 and 80 times per minute). The rate for children is even faster (possibly 100 times per minute).

Airway blocked

What could block the airway? Obviously something like a plastic bag (or even a large sweet or other object) could do this. Another possibility is food that has been vomited.

These can be removed quite easily – for example use a finger to clear the mouth . . . but be careful with small children, only put your finger in the mouth if you can see the obstruction and there is no danger of pushing it down the throat.

If you cannot see the obstruction then treat as for choking (see page 63).

If the casualty is unconscious, the tongue might have fallen to the back of the mouth and be blocking the airway like this:

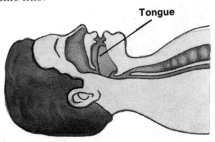

Tongue

Look at that diagram and see where the tongue is. Now look at the two drawings below (where the tongue is not marked) and work out which position would ensure that the tongue fell clear of the airway.

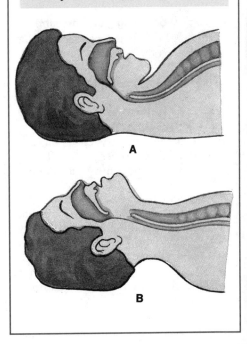

A

B

You can see that the answer was B.

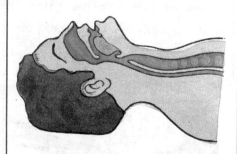

To open the airway:
Lift the chin forward with the index and middle fingers of one hand while pressing the forehead backwards with the heel of the other hand. Opening the airway in this way is essential for anyone who is not breathing. Simply doing this could let the person breathe for himself.

Person not breathing (pulse present)

If the person does not breathe for himself then he will die . . . unless you help.

The way to help is to breathe into the other person's lungs.

This works because the air you breathe out contains more than sufficient unused oxygen. You can blow that into the other person. This is called **Mouth-to-Mouth Ventilation**.

The general stages are:
Open the airway. Clear anything that is obviously in the way. Loosen any tight clothing round the neck. Open your mouth wide, take a deep breath, pinch the person's nostrils together and put your lips around the mouth.

Looking along the chest, blow until you see the chest rise fully.

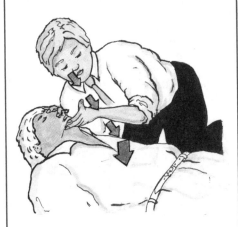

Move your mouth away from the casualty, finish breathing out and watch the chest fall.

When the casualty's chest falls, take in fresh air and repeat the process. Continue breathing at a rate of about 10 breaths per minute for an adult. If you need to leave the casualty to fetch help, give 10 breaths before doing so.

Now think about these questions:

What is the obvious feature which will make the procedure different for children?
What might you do differently?

Children are smaller – they have smaller lungs and faces so you would blow less air into the lungs and you might cover the mouth and *nose* with your mouth. You can see that in this picture:

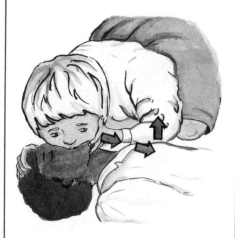

With anyone who has, for example, wounds round the mouth you will have to block the mouth with your finger and blow into the person's nose (cover it with your mouth).

You must keep on breathing for the person until qualified help arrives or someone takes over from you. Do not give up, the person may recover even after needing a long session of this artificial ventilation.

When the casualty does start breathing he may remain unconscious (and so the tongue could still fall back and block the airway or he may vomit).

In order to ensure that the person is safe, you should place him in the *recovery position*. This position lets the person breathe easily.

Look at this diagram of the head and you will see other advantages of the recovery position:

What happens to the tongue?
What will happen to any vomit?

*Details of courses are on page 68.

The tongue falls clear of the airway. Vomit will run clear and so there is no risk of blocking the airway.

Let us look in more detail at how to place someone in this position. Kneel beside the casualty, remove any spectacles and straighten the legs. Place the near arm out at right angles to his body, elbow bent, palm uppermost. Bring the far arm across the chest and hold hand, palm outwards, against near cheek. With your other hand, grasp far thigh and pull knee up, keeping foot flat on ground. Keeping his hand pressed against his cheek, pull at thigh to roll him towards you onto his side. Tilt head back to keep airway open and adjust hand under cheek, if necessary, to maintain position. Adjust upper leg if necessary, so that hip and knee are bent at right angles.

There are some general points about the recovery position:
Lay the person on the *injured* side if there is a chest injury or there is bleeding from inside the ear.

You must always use the recovery position when you are dealing with an unconscious person.

THERE IS NO SUBSTITUTE FOR PROPER TRAINING

Now think about this situation:

A child is drowning, you are in the water, what would you do?

If she has stopped breathing, you would:

Make safe
Lift her head clear of the water.

Emergency Aid
Open the airway.

Apply mouth-to-mouth ventilation.

Notice two things:
1. You would start the treatment as soon as possible, in this case while you are still in the water and making your way to the side of the pool.

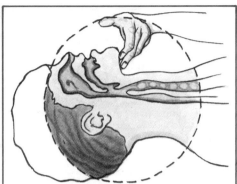

Clear and open the airway

2. **Do not** waste time trying to get water out of her lungs or stomach. Water in the stomach will be vomited when she starts breathing.

Apply artificial ventilation. (Do 2 full breaths checking that the chest is rising, then continue at the normal rate.)

When the casualty is breathing normally, place in the recovery position.

Summary

Let us summarize this section on the airway and breathing:

Assess the situation *and* make it safe.

You may find it unpleasant or distressing to think of actually doing or practising, for example, mouth-to-mouth ventilation. We hope that the dreadful thought of watching a child die, and being unable to help will make you overcome your natural feelings.

Circulation

So far we have looked at three possible causes of deaths:
Mouth and nose blocked: airway blocked and *no breathing*.

Now you will learn what to do if the *heart stops beating*.

One essential point is that a person's heart *can* occasionally be restarted and another point is that you can force blood to be pumped round the body even if the heart has stopped.

This technique **does work** and can be done by anyone. As with artificial ventilation you should practice it *but only under qualified supervision and never on a real person.**

The name of the technique is **Chest Compression.**

The first thing you have to do is check whether the person's heart *is* beating. We have already shown you how to check the pulse in the neck.

---

*Details of St. John Ambulance courses are on page 68.

21

Make sure an ambulance has been sent for. If you have no helper, you must dial 999 before treating the casualty.

The next thing you need to know is *where* the heart is!

Look at this drawing and work out where the centre of his heart will be:

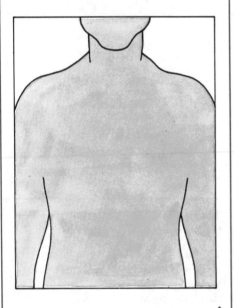

THERE IS NO SUBSTITUTE FOR PROPER TRAINING

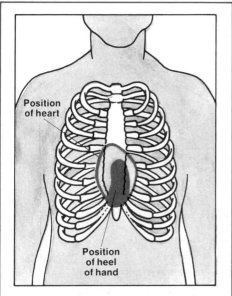

The centre of his heart is marked here:

You will need to press down on the lower half of the breast bone – to find the exact spot you should put the heel of your hand on the centre of the lower half of the breastbone.

Place the heel of your other hand on top and interlock your fingers, like this:

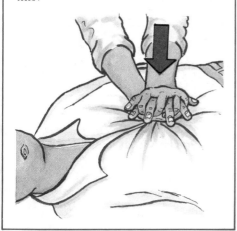

Keep your arms straight and vertical and press the breastbone down about 40 to 50 mm ($1\frac{1}{2}$ to 2 in.) for an adult.

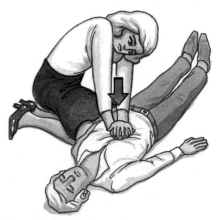

Move back to release the pressure.

With a child you obviously need to use less pressure, place one hand over the *centre* of the breastbone. Press down about 25 to 35 mm (1 to $1\frac{1}{2}$ in.).

Think about this, should you keep on regularly compressing the chest in this way without varying the procedure?

If you *just* perform Chest Compression then no oxygen will enter the lungs. You must perform a regular cycle of Chest Compression along with artificial ventilation.

For an adult, the cycle is 15 chest compressions (at about 80/minute) followed by two breaths of artificial ventilation, another 15 compressions, another 2 breaths and so on. For a child or young baby the cycle is 5 chest compressions to 1 breath.

If there is a second person who is able to give Emergency Aid then the two of you should work as a team. One gives Chest Compressions at about 80/minute with a pause after every 5 compressions to allow the lungs to inflate, whilst the other gives a breath on the upstroke of the fifth compression.

This technique is hard work but *you must not give up*.

Now think about this situation:

You are with a colleague in the staffroom when suddenly he goes pale, grasps his chest then slumps to the ground.

Precisely what should you do?

Assess
Is he breathing? Is his heart beating?

Make safe
Clear the airway (remove any obvious foreign matter, for example, loose teeth which might get in the way).

Emergency Aid
Open the airway. *If he is not breathing and there is no pulse, send for an ambulance.*

Lay him flat on the floor.

Give 2 full breaths of artificial ventilation. Place the heel of the hand about three quarters of the way down the breast-bone.

Place the heel of your other hand on top.

Interlock your fingers (keeping them off the chest).

Press down with straight arms.

Release.

Repeat 15 times (at 80/minute).

Give two breaths of mouth-to-mouth ventilation.

Repeat the cycle until the ambulance crew is ready to take over.

Do not imagine that a heart attack or something similar is the only reason for the heart stopping. A child who has stopped breathing (like the girl who was drowning in the earlier example) might need Chest Compression. A person who is electrocuted will also need this treatment. In fact there are many situations which could result in your having to save someone's life like this.

Look at this picture, what would you have to do?

Assess
The girl seems to have had an electric shock from the typewriter. Is it safe to check her breathing and heartbeat?

Make safe
Turn off the power or stand on some dry paper or thick cloth and use, say a wooden chair to push her free.

Emergency Aid
Check breathing and pulse.
Apply artificial ventilation and Chest Compression as necessary.
As this was not a heart attack (see page 65) place her in the recovery position if/when breathing and heartbeat return. Keep checking breathing and heartbeat.

Inform
You would probably have already sent one of her classmates to get help but remember that you obviously need to report the accident in the usual way.

Summary
Here is a summary of this section on restarting the heart:

Assess the situation and make it safe. Lay him flat on the floor.

Finally, make certain that the casualty is taken to hospital and inform whoever needs to know.

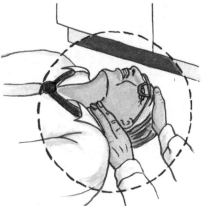

Check the heartbeat by taking the carotid pulse.

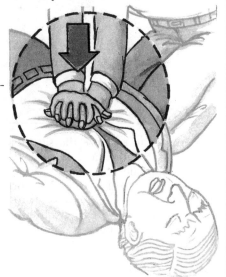

If necessary, give Chest Compression and mouth-to-mouth ventilation.

THERE IS NO SUBSTITUTE FOR PROPER TRAINING

Bleeding

This is another potential cause of death – depending on the severity of the bleeding, it is probable that you quickly could stop (or at least slow down) the loss of blood. In this section you will read about Emergency Aid for both external and internal bleeding.

External bleeding

This can obviously be fairly dramatic (and unpleasant) for both the casualty and you. The treatment, however, is straightforward. You should never apply any sort of tourniquet. Instead, if blood is leaking from a wound you should simply cover the wound with a dressing and press on the wound with your fingers or squeeze the sides of the wound together and keep hold. That technique is called direct pressure. Pressure has to be kept on for at least 5 minutes and possibly up to 15 minutes or even longer to give the blood time to clot.

Gravity can also be used to reduce the amount of blood flowing to a wound, for example an injured arm should be raised to slow down bleeding (unless there is a fracture).

Now think carefully about this question:

If there is a large piece of glass or metal in the wound, should you remove it?

The answer is *no* because it could actually be doing a useful job by helping to block an injured blood vessel – pulling it out could make the bleeding worse. Foreign bodies like this should only be removed at hospital.

What you should do is squeeze the edges of the wound together alongside the object and build up a ring of pads around it.

With any type of wound, if the pad you have used becomes soaked with blood then **do not** remove it, instead you should place another pad on top and use a bit more pressure.

When the bleeding does eventually stop, you should bandage over the pad (or pads) firmly. Notice that this means that where you have built up a ring of pads around a foreign body you will have to criss-cross the bandage around the object.

Finally you must arrange for qualified help and *inform* as necessary.

Let us see how those actions should be applied in this accident.

In this domestic science class someone has cut her hand badly. Blood is spurting out and seems to be spreading everywhere.

What should you do?

Assess
There seems to be a lot of blood – but is it as bad as it seems? A little blood goes a long way, particularly if it mixes with water or some other liquid. In this case the girl is not badly injured . . . but you must still act.

Make safe
Someone could forget that the cooker is switched on and that could cause another accident. You should turn it off.

Emergency Aid
Apply direct pressure to the wound, squeezing the edges together, preferably over a dressing.

Raise the girl's hand.
Put a pad over the wound, still keeping up the pressure and bandage firmly.
Get her to sit down, she is unlikely to be losing so much blood that it will affect the vital organs but at least she will be more comfortable and less likely to faint.
If the pad becomes soaked with blood, press another one on top and bandage it in position.

Inform
You probably would have already sent for help but you should also carry out the normal procedure to record that there has been an accident.

That accident was fairly minor – but suppose you were in a workshop and something really horrifying occurred.

Imagine that you are on the scene when a child has an accident with a chisel, it pierces the boy's arm.

Could you cope?
What should you do?

Assess
This is obviously a major accident and help must be called while you carry out the emergency aid.

Make safe
You must (of course) stop all other activities in the area.

Emergency Aid
If the chisel is firmly embedded in the arm you must *not* pull it out or move it in any way, except to support the weight.
You should lay the boy down.
You should squeeze the edges of the wound against the object (applying direct pressure).
You should press pads around it, adding additional pads when the others become soaked with blood.
You should raise the legs.

Inform
One other important point about emergency aid for bleeding is that you must always remember to check breathing and heartbeat. If they stop you must act immediately (see pages 14 and 22).

Internal bleeding

If internal bleeding occurs then blood may start to collect in the body's cavities or muscles. It may eventually come out of one of the body openings (for example the mouth). In other words, blood is lost from the circulatory system and so cannot carry oxygen to the brain and other vital organs.

If someone has been crushed or had a bad fall, then it is possible that internal bleeding will occur although the effects may not be recognized for some time.

If you were waiting for a doctor to come to someone who had, for example, broken his thigh (and so had internal bleeding)

Which of these statements would probably describe his pulse. What action should you take?

(a) Normal speed but stronger than usual.
(b) Fast and strong.
(c) Slow and strong.
(d) Normal speed and weak.
(e) Slow and weak.
(f) Fast and weak.

The pulse would be fast and weak. (f). *Fast* because the body would be striving to pump blood to the vital organs and *weak* because there is less blood and thus the walls of the arteries would not be pushed out so much as normal when the blood surges through.

You should:

Assess
He obviously needs medical help, you might guess that he had internal bleeding but you would not know for sure. He is breathing and does have a pulse of sorts.

Make safe
He is the only one in danger and so he must quickly be given the right Emergency Aid.

Emergency Aid
You obviously cannot apply direct pressure so you must just do all you can to minimise shock (see page 35). Keep checking the breathing and heartbeat.

Inform
You will already have sent for help so you must just carry out the appropriate actions as laid down in your school's procedure.

Bleeding tooth socket
Another major problem experienced in schools is a tooth socket that continues to bleed after a visit to the dentist.

Emergency Aid
Get the casualty to bite on a pad for at least 10 minutes. If this fails then refer them back to the dentist.

Accidental teeth damage or loss
The successful outcome of treatment of accidents in which teeth are damaged often depends upon the correct first aid being applied and the speedy referral to a dentist for appropriate treatment.

If a blow is severe enough, a tooth or teeth can be knocked out completely. Try to put it back into the socket and get the casualty to bite gently on a pad of gauze or a handkerchief. Arrange for immediate referral to a dentist. If it is not possible put the tooth back in its socket, place it in a cup of milk and send it with the casualty to the dentist. The tooth should be handled gently by the crown only – do not touch the root.

A delay of over 4 hours severely reduces the chance of re-implanting the tooth successfully, so speed is of essence.

Summary

Here is a summary of this section on bleeding.

Assess the situation.
Make safe.
Check breathing and heartbeat.

For external bleeding, apply direct pressure. Press pads onto the wound, add more pads if necessary. Bandage the pads into place. Raise the wound if possible.

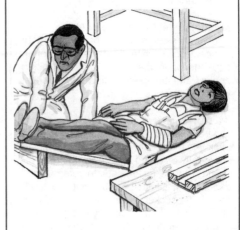

Get the person to lie down with (if other injuries permit) the legs raised.

Finally inform people as necessary and, particularly if the person has possible internal injuries or has been unconscious, make certain that the casualty goes to hospital.

Shock

This is a condition which produces similar effects to internal bleeding.

Shock is caused by loss of some type of fluid from the body – resulting in a smaller volume of blood to carry oxygen. Examples of emergencies which are likely to cause shock include: external or internal bleeding; prolonged vomiting or diarrhoea; extensive burns.

A similar state can be produced by extreme pain or fear (because blood collects in the abdomen or legs).

The body's defence mechanism is to try to keep sufficient blood going to the brain and vital organs . . . at the expense of, for example, the skin or muscles. A person suffering from shock will therefore become cold, pale and weak.

As the heart is working hard, pumping less fluid around but trying to keep up the supply of oxygen, the pulse will become fast and weak.

As with internal bleeding it is essential to help the heart to supply blood to the brain, so similar Emergency Aid is called for:

Depending on other injuries, you should get the person to lie down with the legs raised.

You should prevent the casualty cooling . . . but do not warm the person as too much heat will cause blood to come to the surface of the skin instead of flowing to the vital organs.

In the example below, the young girl has fallen down some stairs.

You assess the situation and find that she is conscious, however, her pulse is rather fast and weak.

You tell her to stay lying quietly where she is until medical help or a qualified First Aider arrives. She says she feels cold.

Which of the following things would you use to help warm her? (You can use more than one, if you wish.)

(a) Electric heater.
(b) Blankets over her.
(c) Blankets under her.
(d) Hot sweet drink.

(a) An electric heater should *not* be used because it would warm the skin too much.

(b) Blankets *over* the girl would be helpful.

(c) Blankets *under* the girl would be even more valuable as the body would lose more heat to the ground than to the air. Remember, however, that you must not move a conscious casualty if there is the slightest risk of spinal injuries.

(d) Drinks (of any sort) MUST NEVER be given to a casualty except in the special cases mentioned elsewhere in this book.

In this case there was an obvious cause for the shock but a similar state can be produced by, for example, a fright.

Summary

This short but important section on shock can be summarised as follows:

Lay the casualty down with (if injuries allow) the legs raised.

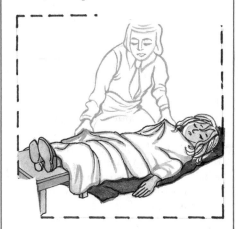

Keep the person warm with blankets, coats and so on. Use them *under* as well as over the person as long as there is no risk of spinal injuries.

Finally inform other people as necessary.

Assess the situation.
Make safe.
Check breathing and heartbeat.

(See also "Fainting" on page 61).

Unconsciousness

In everyday use we normally think of "unconsciousness" as a condition in which the casualty does not react at all. Technically, however, there is a method of assessing levels of responsiveness which relates to whether or not the brain is working normally. A casualty might be on any one of the levels and then may slip quickly to a different level.

Levels of response are assessed in the following manner:

Check:

Eyes
- are they open
- do they open on command
- do they respond to pain
- do they remain closed

Movement: Does the casualty
- move on command
- respond to pain
- make no response

Speech: Is the casualty's response
- normal
- confused
- inappropriate
- incomprehensible
- no response

There are many potential causes of unconsciousness including a head injury, fainting, asphyxia, heart attack, stroke, epilepsy, shock, diabetes and poisoning (including the abuse of alcohol, solvents or drugs).

In Emergency Aid an estimate of the level of responsiveness is important when you are assessing the situation. A casualty who is drowsy might still be able to tell you something important and changes in the level of responsiveness can give valuable information to the doctor later.

Imagine that you are supervising an examination when one of the pupils faints.

What should you do?

Assess
All you know is that a child is unconscious. You must check whether he is still breathing and whether there is a heartbeat.

Make safe
Is the airway open? Do you need to use mouth-to-mouth ventilation or is he breathing normally?
Do you need to use Chest Compression?

Emergency Aid
You should loosen any tight clothing around his chest and neck and place him in the recovery position (see page 17). Act to minimise shock.

Inform
You should already have sent for help, now you must carry out the usual procedures.

The importance of this example is to stress that breathing and heartbeat are your first priority.

You can give adequate Emergency Aid to an unconscious casualty without knowing exactly what is wrong . . . although this information is obviously helpful. The cause of the accident might be obvious or there could be clues such as a warning bracelet. If you decide that it is safe to examine the casualty then follow the stages opposite.

Stage 1 – Check that the airway is open and that the person is breathing.

Stage 2 – Check that there is a heartbeat.

Stage 3 – Move the person as little as possible and be gentle, check for obvious bleeding.

Stage 4 – Start at the head and work down to the feet, checking over and under the person
(a) for dampness which could indicate bleeding and
(b) for fractures.

Look at the drawing on the next page:

THERE IS NO SUBSTITUTE FOR PROPER TRAINING

Here a boy has been accidentally knocked unconscious, you have carried out stages 1 to 4, the casualty is breathing normally and there is no bleeding.

Having sent for help, what should you do next?

You should gently roll him into the recovery position moving his head, trunk and legs simultaneously. If possible you should put some warm, dry material (such as a tracksuit) on the ground underneath him. If more warm materials are available, these should be placed over him.

You must stay with the casualty and keep checking his breathing and heartbeat.

N.B. If there is any possibility of spinal injury do not move the casualty unless difficulty in breathing makes it vital.

Summary – Unconsciousness

You should assess the situation and make safe.
Check breathing and heartbeat.

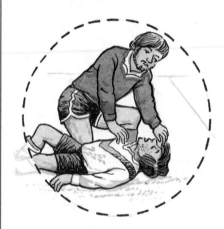

Carefully check for serious bleeding which needs action.

Place the casualty in the recovery position.
Keep the person warm with blankets or clothing under and over him.
Keep checking airway, breathing and heartbeat.

Inform people in the usual way.

Poisons, Drugs and Alcohol abuse, Glue sniffing, Foreign Bodies

If you swallow, inhale or absorb through the skin anything that affects the correct working of the body, then you are *poisoned*. The Emergency Aid is the *same* whatever the substance involved. Thus a child can be *poisoned* by swallowing tablets, corrosive poisons or alcohol, by inhaling gases or solvents, by injecting himself or even by being bitten by a snake.

Remember, the Emergency Aid is the same:

IF THE CHILD IS UNCONSCIOUS:

Check airway, breathing and heart-beat (see pages 12–14).
If breathing is normal, loosen tight clothing around the neck and chest and place in the RECOVERY POSITION.

If breathing has stopped apply artificial ventilation.*
Get qualified help.
Find out as many facts about the situation as you can.

IF THE CHILD IS CONSCIOUS:
Ask the child what happened – he may lose consciousness.
Assess the situation and make it safe (e.g. take away any poisonous substances).
Do not make the child vomit.
Get qualified help.
If there are burns around the mouth, give sips of water.
Keep the child warm and quiet and under observation in case he becomes unconscious.

---

*Protect yourself from chemicals around the lips by washing them off or blowing through a cloth.

43

Imagine that you are with a group of pupils on an overseas trip. One evening you see a group of three or four teenagers, one is being supported by the others who smell of alcohol. He falls to the ground.

What should you do?

If he is unconscious, immediately provide the usual Emergency Aid for unconsciousness.

Emergency Aid
If he is breathing normally, loosen tight clothing around the neck and chest and place him in the recovery position (see also page 16).

Inform
He needs medical treatment, so get qualified help. Whilst it is arriving find out as many facts surrounding his condition as possible.

Here is another example of poisoning:

After lunchbreak one day a girl complains of feeling unwell and of blurred vision. Her friends tell you that she has been sniffing glue. She may have sores around her lips and nose.

What should you do?

This is the Emergency Aid you should provide:

If she has any glue, polythene bags etc. still in her possession, take them away.
Get qualified help.
Keep her quiet and warm.
Make sure that she is observed closely as she may become unconscious before help arrives. (Then treat as above.)

Foreign bodies

Young children in particular are likely to swallow small objects, or insert an item in an ear or the nose.

In general there is no real emergency and your action should just be to seek medical help or remove the child to hospital. (See also "Choking" on page 63.)

Foreign bodies in the eye, however, need immediate action.

If the foreign body is:

(a) on the coloured part of the eye,
(b) embedded in the eye, or
(c) stuck to the eye

then do not try to remove it. Your actions should be to:

Tell the casualty not to rub or move the eye.

Cover the eye with a clean, non-fluffy pad, and remove the casualty to hospital.

If the foreign body is *not* on the coloured part of the eye and is not stuck or embedded, then you should be able to remove it quite easily.

First you must assess the situation so ask the person to sit facing the light, stand behind and hold the chin steady with one hand while you use the thumb for forefinger of the other hand to separate the eyelids.

Ask the casualty to look right, left, up and down (this will enable you to see every part of the eye).

> **Having seen where the foreign body is what action should you take?**

You should try to wash the foreign body away from the eye, making certain that water drains off the face and not into the other eye.

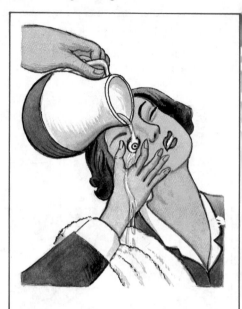

If the foreign body does not wash away (*and is not stuck or embedded*) then lift it off with, for example, the corner of a clean dampened handkerchief.

If the foreign body is under the upper lid then ask the person to look down. Take hold of the eyelashes and pull the upper lid downwards and out, over the lower lid. The lower eyelashes will probably brush the object off.

If you fail to remove the foreign body then cover the eye with a non-fluffy pad and seek medical help.

Summary

Poisons and foreign bodies

Assess the situation and make safe.
Check breathing and heartbeat.
Do not turn yourself into another casualty.

Carry out the appropriate Emergency Aid, keeping the casualty calm and still.

If necessary carry out the emergency aid for chemical burns of the mouth or the eye (see pages 54 and 55).

Keep checking the casualty's breathing and heartbeat, and act to minimise shock.

Inform people in the usual way.

THERE IS NO SUBSTITUTE FOR PROPER TRAINING

Burns and Scalds

Burns and scalds can cause serious disabilities, your prompt and correct action in an emergency could reduce suffering.

The Emergency Aid for burns is based on the simple fact that heat does the damage and so you must immediately cool down the affected area.

Over the next few pages are some specific actions for different situations and types of burn – but let us start by considering a fairly minor accident.

Minor burns

This child has touched a hot part of a cooker and has a small burn on her finger.

Which of the following is the correct Emergency Aid?

(a) Apply a sterile adhesive plaster.
(b) Put butter on the burn to soothe the pain.
(c) Do nothing.
(d) Hold her hand under cold water.

(a) You should *not* cover the burn with an adhesive plaster.
(b) You should *not* apply any type of grease or ointment (it will not cool the burn and will make it more difficult to clean).
(c) You must give the correct Emergency Aid – even though the girl's finger is away from the cooker, her finger is still hot and so the burn will get worse.
(d) The best Emergency Aid is to hold the burn under cold water (or any other cold, harmless liquid) for at least 10 minutes.

The general Emergency Aid for burns is therefore based on common-sense – you use cold water to cool the skin.

Severe burns

At a more serious incident you might have to carry out other actions, for example, extinguish burning clothes, before you can deal with the actual burns.
Look at this drawing:

The Bunsen burner has set fire to the boy's lab coat. You must obviously extinguish the flames.

But how?

Should you:

(a) roll the boy on the ground,
(b) wrap him in a coat or blanket, or
(c) throw water over him?

One essential point is that you *must* force the person to lie down rather than panicking and rushing about. You might even have to drag the casualty to the ground.

You should not roll him on the ground as this might cause the flames to spread.

If you have a bucket of water *immediately* available then you could use this, but you must not waste time finding one.

The best answer is probably "wrap him in a coat or blanket" – provided that the blanket is not of man made fibre and so will not melt (and **do not** use a "cellular" one). You should use anything suitable which is immediately available to smother the flames.

Another advantage of using, for example, a blanket is that you shield yourself from the flames as you approach the casualty.

So far then you have *assessed* the situation and *made it safe* (although that Bunsen burner needs to be turned off as soon as possible).

The actual emergency aid for a severe burn would be to pour water gently over the burned area for at least 10 minutes.

Gently remove any watches, rings, belts or tight clothing before any swelling occurs. **Do not** remove anything that is sticking to a burn.

The next stage is to cover the burn.

Remembering that you must try to reduce the risk of infection as well as trying not to cause unnecessary pain, now think about this question:

> **What essential feature must you look for in anything you intend to use to cover a burn?**

The cloth must be *clean* and it must *not* be fluffy (threads might stick to the burn). A clean plastic bag or kitchen film makes a good dressing for burns.

As with small burns, you must not apply any creams, fats or ointments:
you must not break any blisters,
remove any loose skin,
or interfere with the injury in any way.

If a limb is badly burnt you should immobilise it.

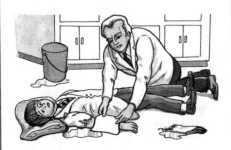

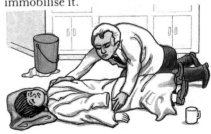

Fluid loss from extensive burns would cause shock (see page 35) and you would need to guard against it.

If the casualty is conscious, then you can help to replace the lost fluid by giving sips of cold water (*nothing else*) at frequent intervals.

Scalds

Having been told the Emergency Aid to carry out for minor and severe burns you would probably know what to do in the following situation.

Here a child has been scalded rather than burnt.
What would you do?

Assess
It is obvious that the child has been scalded – but is the liquid just water?

Make safe
The Bunsen burner must be turned off and you must carry out the correct Emergency Aid ... *quickly.*

Emergency Aid
As with minor burns, your first priority is to cool the area by immersing in cold water for at least 10 minutes.

Remove anything which may become tight as swelling occurs.
Make the casualty comfortable, immobilising any seriously scalded area.

Try to prevent infection by covering the area with a clean, non-fluffy cloth.
Also you must guard against shock (see page 35).

Inform
You will already have sent for help – your final action will be to carry out the normal procedure for reporting an accident.

Burns in the mouth and throat

A scald from drinking very hot liquid or the effects of breathing very hot air (for example by someone who has escaped from a fire) can be very serious. The inside of the throat could swell, blocking the airway and thus stopping the person from breathing. The casualty will also, of course, be in great pain.

Look at this situation:

You have *assessed* the situation and *made it safe* (possibly a quick warning to the others).

What Emergency Aid would you provide?

You should loosen any tight clothing around the neck then (because the person is conscious) give sips of cold water at frequent intervals.

If breathing stops then open the airway and use mouth-to-mouth ventilation. If the person's heartbeat stops then you must also use external chest compression.

If the person becomes unconscious but is breathing normally then you should use the recovery position.

Your last action, for the moment, is to minimise the risk of shock (see page 35).

Having carried out this Emergency Aid you would need to keep checking the casualty's breathing until an ambulance or other medical help arrived.

Chemical burns

There are many chemicals which will cause burns; they are found not just in Science Laboratories but also wherever cleaning fluids, bleaches, paint strippers, garden chemicals and so on might be used or stored.

The Emergency Aid for chemical burns is very much the same as for scalds:
Flood the affected area with cold water for at least 10 minutes to prevent further damage to the burned tissue. (Try to use slowly running water and make sure that it drains away safely from undamaged areas as it will be contaminated.)

At the same time gently remove any contaminated clothing but make sure that you **do not** turn yourself into a casualty by getting the chemical on your own skin.

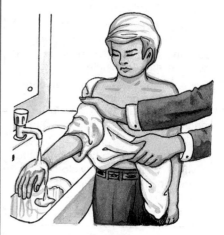

Remove anything which may become tight.

Make the casualty comfortable, immobilising any badly burned area.

Try to prevent infection by covering the area with a clean, non-fluffy cloth. Guard against shock.

Think about this question:
A child has swallowed some corrosive chemical.

What could you do to relieve the pain?

As with ordinary burns in the mouth and throat you could give frequent sips of cold water as long as the child is conscious. (See also page 43 – Poisons.)

Chemical burns in the eye

The same principle applies as for other burns . . . you must quickly use cold, gently running water to wash away the substance. There is an important point to bear in mind about the contaminated water which is running away, however. That is that it *must* drain off the face without contacting the uninjured eye.

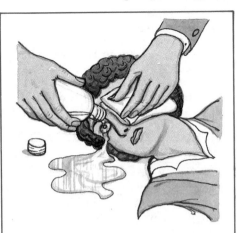

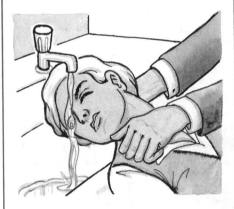

You must check that both surfaces of the eyelids have been well washed (you may need to pull the eyelids open – be firm but gentle).

An alternative method of cleansing the eye would be:

(1) to get the child to put that side of the face in a bowl of cold water and blink,

(2) to sit or lay the person down with the head tilted towards the injured side (whilst protecting the uninjured side). The eyelid should then be gently opened and clean water poured over it.

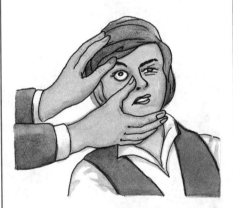

You should now cover the eye with clean, non-fluffy cloth and ensure that the appropriate people are informed of the accident.

There is one last point about this type of accident: *do not let the casualty rub the eye.*

Electrical burns

These might seem to be fairly minor but actually will probably be deep. The actual Emergency Aid will be as for other severe burns – the difference being at the earlier stage of "making safe".

You must not turn yourself into another casualty. Switch off the electricity or, as in the picture below where a colleague has received an electric shock from an overhead projector, stand on some insulating material (such as dry paper) and use, for example, a wooden chair to push the casualty away before you try to give any treatment.

Apart from the burns, it is possible that the person's breathing and even heartbeat will stop, so (when it is safe) you may need to do mouth-to-mouth ventilation and Chest Compression.

Summary

The Emergency Aid for burns and scalds is summarised in two parts.

Minor burns, scalds, burns in mouth and throat, chemical burns

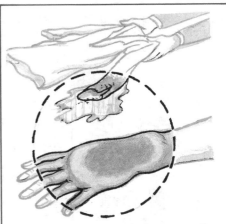

Assess the situation and make it safe. Check breathing and heartbeat.

Take off any contaminated or hot, soaked clothing.
Remove anything which will become tight as swelling occurs.

Finally, inform people as necessary.

The Emergency Aid for electrical and other severe burns is summarised on the next page.

Cool the area for at least 10 minutes.

Severe burns (including electrical burns)

Assess the situation, and make it safe – but do not turn yourself into another casualty.
Check breathing and heartbeat.

Make the person as comfortable as possible, immobilise a badly burned limb.

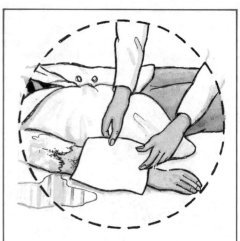

Cover the area with a clean, non-fluffy cloth.
Try to minimise shock.

With all burns

Do not apply fats, creams or lotions to a burn.
Do not touch the burn.
Do not break blisters or remove loose skin.
Do not turn yourself into another casualty.
If breathing and heartbeat stop then *immediately* open the airway, and begin artificial ventilation and Chest Compression.

Finally, inform people as necessary.

Specific Emergencies

In your professional relationships with pupils and their families you are likely to gather facts which could be useful if you are faced with an emergency. Some people may still be embarrassed about medical conditions from which they or their children suffer. However, you would normally be forewarned that one of the children in your class was diabetic or had had an epileptic fit.

Other specific emergencies which are covered in this chapter include fainting and choking.

Over the next few pages we will consider various situations where you should act, in each case you will be given some facts about the condition together with the Emergency Aid which is necessary.

Minor epilepsy

These fits may even be unnoticed because the casualty just appears to be daydreaming, staring ahead blankly. Other possible symptoms include loss of memory and chewing, smacking the lips, fiddling with clothing or other strange behaviour.

Emergency Aid
Do nothing except protect the person from any danger. Keep other people away and talk quietly to the casualty.

Inform
The casualty should see a doctor. Inform other people as appropriate.

Major epilepsy

Suppose one of your older pupils has a major epileptic attack where he or she loses consciousness and falls to the ground, goes rigid and then, after a few seconds, starts to jerk violently.

Bearing in mind the Emergency Aid for minor epilepsy.

What should you do?

You should do nothing except protect the casualty in the following ways.

Emergency Aid
Try to protect the person, for example by breaking the fall.
Clear spectators away.
If possible, carefully loosen clothing around the neck.
When the convulsions stop, place the person in the Recovery Position.
Stay with the casualty until recovery is complete.

Do not try to restrain the casualty.
Do not move the person unless he or she is in danger.
Do not try to open the mouth or place anything in it (even if the tongue has been bitten).
Do not try to wake the casualty.
Do not give the casualty anything to drink until he or she is *fully* alert.

Inform
The person should tell his or her doctor about this latest attack.
Inform other people as appropriate.
It is likely that the casualty wears a warning locket or bracelet or carries an orange card stating that he or she is liable to epileptic fits.

Asthma
Symptoms and signs
Note: person may be very anxious and have difficulty in breathing out and have blueness of face.

Emergency Aid
Reassure and calm the person.
Get the person to sit down and lean forward resting on a support.
Provide good supply of air.
Let casualty take any medication they have to treat an attack.

Inform
Seek further medical help.

Diabetes

Diabetes arises when the body cannot adequately regulate the concentration of sugar in the blood. Many diabetics carry warning cards or wear warning bracelets or lockets. The condition is normally controlled by balancing the diet against insulin injections or tablets.

A problem will arise if the concentration of sugar in the blood unexpectedly falls (due to the person missing a meal or burning up the sugar during exercise, for example). This imbalance could also occur if too much insulin has been taken, again causing low blood sugar.

Unconsciousness can result.

If one of your pupils who is diabetic starts to go pale and sweat or appears confused and disorientated or aggressive, what Emergency Aid should you provide?

Emergency Aid

The problem is caused by lack of sugar, so (provided that the person is conscious and able to swallow) immediately give something sugary. *Be warned,* many modern foods contain artificial sweetners which will not work. You must use something containing actual sugar.
In the rare circumstances of the casualty becoming unconscious (but breathing normally), place in the Recovery Position and carry out the general Emergency Aid for unconsciousness (see page 40).

Inform

The casualty must go to hospital and you must inform other people in the usual way.

Fainting

This is another condition which was mentioned earlier in the book. It is caused by a temporary reduction in the flow of blood to the brain. If people are standing still for long periods then gravity might cause a large volume of blood to collect in the lower part of the body.

If you are with a group of children who have to stand for some time, you might wish to suggest that they flex their leg muscles and toes to help circulation.

Emergency Aid

It may help to sit the casualty down with the head between the knees. Advise her to take deep breaths.

If a child does faint, however, what Emergency Aid should you give?

Raise the legs, loosen any tight clothing at the neck, chest and waist to assist circulation and breathing.
If the person remains drowsy, see that he has plenty of fresh air, fan air onto the face.
If necessary, place in the shade.
Keep checking breathing.
A person who has fainted will start to recover once he is on the ground – if not then you must place in the recovery position and treat for unconsciousness (see pages 17 and 40).

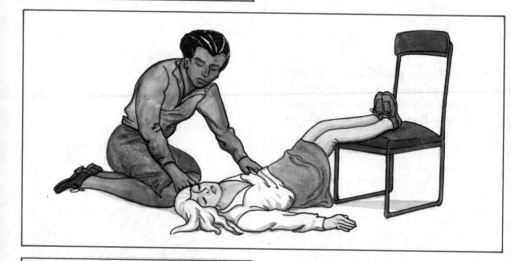

Do not give the casualty any alcohol.
Do not give anything to drink or eat until the person is fully conscious (and then just sips of cold water).

Inform
If you are in any doubt about the casualty's condition, seek qualified help. Inform other people in the usual way.

Choking

A piece of food which "goes the wrong way" can obstruct breathing and is very frightening. In fact, however, the difficulty in breathing is probably caused by a spasm as the person fights to breathe in. Simply coughing may well be sufficient to relieve the spasm and help the person to breathe.

The Emergency Aid for conscious adults and children is shown below:

Adults

Open the airway, remove any obvious debris, false teeth and so on.

Encourage the person to cough. If this does not work then:
Help the person to bend forward with the head lower than the lungs, slap up to five times between the shoulder blades with the *heel* of your hand. Each slap should be firm enough to dislodge the obstruction. Check the mouth, hook the obstruction out if it is visible.

Repeat the backslaps as necessary.

Children

Again encourage the child to cough. If this does not work:
Sit down or kneel on one knee with the child, head down, over the other knee.

Support the chest with one hand and slap between the shoulder blades as before.

If the casualty becomes unconscious, what Emergency Aid should you provide?

Unconscious casualty

Emergency Aid
Open the airway and apply mouth-to-mouth ventilation. If this does not work then pull the casualty onto the side facing you with the chest against your thigh and the head well back.

Slap up to five times with the heel of your hand between the shoulder blades. Check the mouth.

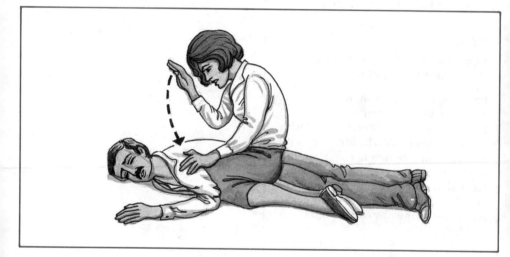

Keep repeating the process.*

Inform
Carry out the usual stages of informing people as necessary.

*There is another technique which should only be used if essential as it can injure the casualty if done incorrectly. Details of St. John courses are on page 68.

Heart attacks

There are three conditions under this heading:

Cardiac Arrest – The heart actually stops beating for some reason.

Coronary Obstruction – A blood clot stops blood reaching part of the heart muscle.

Angina Pectoris – Narrow blood vessels reduce the amount of blood reaching the heart muscle.

Angina Pectoris is usually brought on by exercise or excitement, the attacks normally last only a few minutes. The person may have previously seen a doctor and know how to cope – for example by resting and/or taking special tablets. The casualty will have crushing pain in the chest, the skin may be ashen and the lips blue, the person may be short of breath.

A Coronary obstruction causes similar symptoms to Angina Pectoris but the pain does not go with rest and in addition sweating may develop, the pulse will be fast – becoming weaker and irregular, there may be symptoms of shock, the casualty may become unconscious and breathing and heartbeat may stop.

A Cardiac Arrest is obviously the most serious emergency that you could face, heartbeat and breathing stop, the casualty will be unconscious with ashen skin.

If there is no heartbeat then you must use Chest Compression along with mouth-to-mouth ventilation.

If there is a faint or irregular heartbeat, do you think you should use Chest Compression?

No – You must not use Chest Compression if the casualty's heart is beating.

The correct Emergency Aid for Angina Pectoris and Coronary Obstruction, where the casualty is conscious and the heart has not stopped, is as follows:

Emergency Aid
Help the person to sit and support by placing a jacket or blanket under the knees. Loosen tight clothing round the neck, chest and waist.

If the person becomes unconscious but is breathing normally, place in the recovery position.

If the breathing and heartbeat stop, use Chest Compression and mouth-to-mouth ventilation.

Treat for shock.

Keep checking breathing and heartbeat.

Inform

The casualty must be removed to hospital as quickly as possible. (A person who suffers from Angina Pectoris may have enough experience of the condition to feel that this is unnecessary. If the pains continue, however, they *do* need to go to hospital.)

Other people should be informed in the usual way.

The correct Emergency Aid for Cardiac Arrest, as stated on the previous page, is Chest Compression combined with mouth-to-mouth ventilation (see pages 14 and 23).

Summary

Emergency Aid has four parts:

Assess the situation

For example the boy's forearm in the illustration is at a strange angle.

Make it safe

The boy is conscious and breathing normally. There is no external bleeding. You should not move the casualty.

Emergency Aid

Act to minimise the risk of shock, use blankets or coats to stop the boy getting cold.

Inform

He obviously needs medical attention, in addition you must inform parents and others, using your school's usual procedure.

Do not try to do too much.

In addition to the specific circumstances mentioned in this book, always send the casualty to hospital if you suspect that there are internal injuries or if the person has been unconscious, (except in the case of Epilepsy, see page 60).

Finally, in view of your responsibilities, decide whether you should become a qualified First Aider.

Further Training

This book has provided you with the guidance that you need to give Emergency Aid. It is, however, no real substitute for a proper First Aid course. Artificial Ventilation (page 14), Chest Compression (page 23) *must* be practised under qualified supervision and this is why you are reminded throughout the text that there is 'No substitute for proper training'.

Many Local Education Authorities already organise First Aid courses in partnership with St. John Ambulance and it is worth enquiring whether one is available in your locality. Typically, a group of teachers get together and ask for a course and receive training at their schools from St. John Ambulance Trainers.

Please, then, consider taking a St. John course, the following are offered in all Counties in England and Wales:

Emergency Aid course
(3 hours' instruction)
This is practical training on the topics covered by this book.

Essentials of First Aid course
(16 hours' instruction)
This is a longer course to produce a really effective First Aider.

First Aid at Work course

(24 hours' instruction)

This is a course which leads to the statutory certificate recognised by the Health and Safety Executive, and is additionally a useful extra qualification for *school leavers* who intend to carry out First Aid in the work place as it is valued by employers who, by law, have to provide qualified First Aiders on their premises.

Details of all St. John courses are available in your County. (See Useful Addresses).

The address of St. John Ambulance Headquarters is:

1 Grosvenor Crescent
LONDON SW1X 7EF
(Tel: 071–235 5231)

Useful Addresses

AVON
10 Woodborough Street
EASTON
Bristol BS5 0JB
Tel: 0272 512567

BEDFORDSHIRE
St. John House
34 St John's Street
BEDFORD MK42 0DH
Tel: 0234 216200

BERKSHIRE
Church Road, Woodley
READING RG5 4QN
Tel: 0734 442623

BUCKINGHAMSHIRE
Croft Road
AYLESBURY
Bucks HP21 7RD
Tel: 0296 23886

CAMBRIDGESHIRE
3 Barton Road
CAMBRIDGE CB3 9JZ
Tel: 0223 355334

CHESHIRE
Countess of Chester Hospital
Valley Drive, Liverpool Road
CHESTER CH1 1FA
Tel: 0244 383407

CLEVELAND
11 Cornfield Road
MIDDLESBROUGH
Cleveland TS5 5QJ
Tel: 0642 826723

CORNWALL
Princess Chula House
City Road
TRURO TR1 2JL
Tel: 0872 77867

CUMBRIA
The Strand
BARROW IN FURNESS
LA14 2HG
Tel: 0229 835667

DERBYSHIRE
Alma House
Derby Road
CHESTERFIELD S40 2ED
Tel: 0246 200272

DEVON
Tamar Ward
Langdon Hospital
Exeter Road
DAWLISH
Tel: 0626 888359

DORSET
North Square
DORCHESTER DT1 1HY
Tel: 0305 264510

DURHAM
St. John House
27 Old Elvet
DURHAM DH1 3HN
Tel: 09138 69062

ESSEX
Lancaster House
140 Mildmay Road
CHELMSFORD CM2 0EB
Tel: 0245 355789

GLOUCESTERSHIRE
St. John House
St. George's Place
CHELTENHAM GL50 3PQ
Tel: 0242 513610

GUERNSEY
Baliwick Office
Rohais
ST PETER PORT
Tel: 0481 727129

HAMPSHIRE
St. John House
Worthy Lane
WINCHESTER SO23 7AB
Tel: 0962 863366

HEREFORD & WORCESTER
148 Wylds Way
WORCESTER WR5 1DN
Tel: 0905 359512

HERTFORDSHIRE
102 Ashley Road
ST ALBANS AL1 5DF
Tel: 0727 54333

HUMBERSIDE
Priory House
Popple Street
HULL HU9 1LP
Tel: 0482 588564

ISLE OF MAN
18 Port-e-Chee Avenue
DOUGLAS
Tel: 0624 621615

ISLE OF WIGHT
12 Manners View, Dodner Park
NEWPORT PO33 4HS
Tel: 0983 822794

JERSEY
Midvale Road
ST HELIER
Tel: 0534 35611

KENT
Violet Astor House
41 Church Street
MAIDSTONE ME14 1EL
Tel: 0622 755924

LANCASHIRE
15–17 Mount Street
PRESTON PR1 8AD
Tel: 0772 52239

LEICESTERSHIRE
112 Regent Road
LEICESTER LE1 7LT
Tel: 0533 553954

LINCOLNSHIRE
The Cardinal's Hat
268 High Street
LINCOLN LN2 1JG
Tel: 0522 523701

Gtr LONDON
Edwina Mountbatten House
63 York Street
LONDON W1H 1PS
Tel: 071 258 3456

Gtr MANCHESTER
St. John House
Egerton Road
FALLOWFIELD
Manchester M14 6XX
Tel: 061 2572000

MERSEYSIDE
St Margaret's Parish Centre
Belmont Road, Anfield
LIVERPOOL L6 4AD
Tel: 051 2637300

NORFOLK
59 King Street
NORWICH NR1 1PH
Tel: 0603 621649

NORTHAMPTONSHIRE
33a Billing Road
NORTHAMPTON NN1 5DQ
Tel: 0604 33711

NORTHUMBRIA
St. John House
Grainger Park Road
NEWCASTLE UPON TYNE NE4 8RY
Tel: 091 2737938

NORTH YORKSHIRE
46 Topcliffe Road
SOWERBY
Thirsk YO7 1RB
Tel: 0845 522818

NOTTINGHAMSHIRE
561 Valley Road
BASFORD NG5 1JG
Tel: 0602 784625

OXFORDSHIRE
St. John House
High Street
KIDLINGTON OX5 2DN
Tel: 086–75 78229

SHROPSHIRE
St. John House
Priory Road
SHREWSBURY SY1 1RU
Tel: 0743 231280

SOMERSET
St. John House
60 Staplegrove Road
TAUNTON TA1 1DH
Tel: 0823 337285

SOUTH & WEST YORKSHIRE
St. John Hall
Garden Street
RAVENSTHORPE
Dewsbury WF13 3AR
Tel: 0924 497012

STAFFORDSHIRE
18 Litchfield Road
STAFFORD ST17 4LJ
Tel: 0785 57124/5

SUFFOLK
St. John House
30 Samuel Court
IPSWICH IP4 2EL
Tel: 0473 254005

SURREY
St. John House
Stocton Road
GUILDFORD GU1 1HH
Tel: 0483 67163

SUSSEX
25a Farncombe Road
WORTHING
West Sussex BN11 2AY
Tel: 0903 235599

WARWICKSHIRE
St. John Ambulance Pavilion
National Agricultural Centre
STONELEIGH CV8 2LZ
Tel: 0203 696521

WEST MIDLANDS
Nelson Memorial Hall
100 Lionel Street
BIRMINGHAM B3 1DG
Tel: 021 236 6660

WILTSHIRE
St. John House
St John's Street
DEVIZES SN10 1AT
Tel: 0380 728362

SCOTLAND
St. Andrew's Ambulance Association
Milton Street
GLASGOW
Tel: 041 3324031

WALES
Priory House
Lisvane Road, Llanishen
CARDIFF CF4 5XT
Tel: 0222 750222

NORTHERN IRELAND
Erne Purdysburn Hospital
Saintfield Road
BELFAST BT8 8RA
Tel: 0232 799393

Index

St. John Cadets

St. John Ambulance has Cadet
Divisions throughout the Country
and welcomes boys and girls aged ten
to eighteen years. St. John Cadets
learn First Aid and other subjects and
there are opportunities for adventure
training.

St. John Badgers

Young people aged 6–10 can also
join the Badger movement. This
provides an exciting range of
activities leading to the Super Badger
Award.

The telephone number of your local
Division or Set can be obtained from
County Headquarters. (See page 70).

Teaching Children First Aid
The St. John Ambulance Three Cross Award

More and more teachers in primary and secondary schools throughout the UK are including a simple first aid course in their timetables. It need not take more than a few hours and can be taught as part of a civics or health programme and is particularly useful as a preparation for outdoor trips. To assist teachers to instruct in this important subject St. John Ambulance has available a special low price video which contains three lessons, each of approximately fifteen minutes.

This video pack is part of a scheme called **THE ST. JOHN AMBULANCE THREE CROSS AWARD** and, for a small sum, provides colourful badges and certificates to pupils who can demonstrate to their teachers a knowledge of simple Emergency Aid skills.

There are three standards. One Cross, Two Cross, and Three Cross, suitable for children from nine upwards. Many experts now believe that acquiring Emergency Aid techniques is as important as learning to swim.

Children are usually fascinated by first aid, and this simply administered scheme provides the additional motivation of red, blue and green badges (one for each standard) and colour coded certificates which are signed by the instructor or headteacher.

Full details are included in a comprehensive booklet supplied with each video. Included are teaching objectives, test cards and advice on equipment.

The St. John Ambulance video is presented by Philip Schofield, who is a well-known TV personality.

It has many exciting scenes – an accident on a busy road, a rescue from a river, a scalding scene – and is extremely realistic without being in anyway upsetting.

St. John Ambulance is a charity, hence the fact that this video is about half the price of comparable commercial productions.

An order form and full details are available direct from St. John Supplies, Priory House, St. John's Lane, London EC1M 4DA. Telephone: 071–251 0004. Fax: 071–253 8826.

Notes

Notes

Emergency Index

...urrounding countryside.

Circular walk from Brockweir

4 miles (6.5 km)

The walk starts at Brockweir Bridge **A**. Cross over the bridge and glance upstream, where you can see a small, disused wharf, a reminder of days when trows were both built and traded here. Brockweir itself is a most attractive village with two of the houses showing little Gothic windows, suggesting that the Tintern monks may once have had a grange here. Turn right past the pub **B** and the little Moravian church, and go through a metal gate to join the broad track running parallel to the river. At first it is enclosed by hedges on either side, with glimpses of the river and the occasional view across to Tintern Old Station. Eventually, the track begins to move away from the river and into the woods to begin a steady climb. The area is typical of the broad-leaved woodland that clothes both banks of the river. The climb is gentle and the viewpoint constantly changing.

At a junction of tracks by a stone wall **C** turn back sharply to the left on the path signposted to Devil's Pulpit. Almost immediately, the path

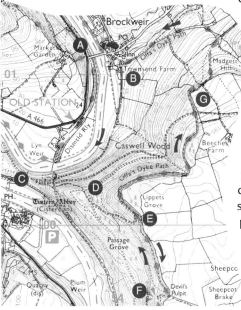

divides. Take the way to the right, on the path that begins to climb rather more steeply, and just beyond this, where there is a second division, turn left onto the path marked by a yellow arrow. The views are lost as the track plunges into dense, dark woodland and steadily steepens. It passes between old, gnarled trees and rocks, and the layered limestone provides a natural staircase. At the top of this sec-

Looking down from the Devil's Pulpit at the tidal waters of the Wye as it flows past Tintern Abbey.

tion a seat has been thoughtfully provided, and here you take the path to the right. The path joins a broad track **D** but immediately turns off again as a narrow path, again waymarked by a yellow arrow. The path zigzags at the top of the hill and finally reaches the rim of the valley **E**.

Turn right on the path signposted to the Devil's Pulpit. This is part of the Offa's Dyke Long-Distance Path, and the dyke itself, which once divided England from Wales, appears as a massive bank and ditch. Just before the stile at the end of the wood turn right and after 100 yards the Pulpit itself appears, a limestone pinnacle **F** that is indeed somewhat pulpit-shaped; below is a quite magnificent view down to the Wye and Tintern Abbey. Retrace your steps to **E** and continue straight on along Offa's Dyke, signposted to Brockweir. The path continues along the edge of the dyke as a comfortable path along the valley rim. A gap in the woods gives another fine view down to Brockweir Bridge. After remaining level for quite a long way, the path begins to descend and where tracks cross you continue straight on. The woods thin out, with fields to the right and ever more open views down to the left. Shortly after the fields appear, look out for a marker post and take the obvious stony path heading diagonally downhill. It emerges from the woods **G** and turns sharply left, and Brockweir Bridge appears dead ahead. Turn right to cross the field, following a line of waymarks, heading in the direction of conifers that spike the far hillside. At the fence turn right to reach a stile, then turn left to take the path downhill beside the fence, and follow the path all the way down to the stables at Brockweir. At the track turn right to return to the start.

USEFUL
INFORMATION

TRANSPORT

Information on transport can be obtained from Tourist Information Centres (see below).

Rail The nearest railway station to the start of the Walk is Llandrindod Wells. Rhayader can be reached from there by bus. There is a station at Chepstow when you reach the other end.

Road It is possible to reach the start of the Walk by coach. Information can be obtained from the relevant county councils:

Gwent County Council, Cwmbran, Gwent NP44 2XF.

Hereford and Worcester County Council, County Hall, Spetchley Road, Worcester WR5 2NP.

Powys County Council, County Hall, Llandrindod Wells, Powys, LD1 5LG. For information on long-distance coaches contact National Express 0990 808080.

ACCOMMODATION

Information on accommodation is available from Tourist Information Centres (see below). This includes bed and breakfast, hotels, bunkhouses and camping. There are also leaflets published by the county councils: Hereford and Worcester County council publishes one annually for the Monmouth to Hay-on-Wye section. This is also available from Tourist Information Centres. There is also an annual publication, *Stilwell's National Trail Companion*, which has a section listing accommodation on the Wye Valley Walk. It is available from Stilwell Publishing Co, The Courtyard, 59 Charlotte Road, Shoreditch, London, EC2A 3QT.

The following youth hostels are on or near the Wye Valley walk:

GR: 162: 523934   Chepstow: Mounton Road, Chepstow, Gwent NP6 6AA (01291 622685).

GR: 162: 508130   Monmouth: Priory Street School, Priory Street, Monmouth, Gwent NP5 3NX (01600 5116).

GR: 162: 591177   Welsh Bicknor: Welsh Bicknor Rectory, Welsh Bicknor, Ross-on-Wye, Herefordshire HR9 6JJ (01594 60300).

*GR: 162: 558045   St Briavels: The Castle, St Briavels, Lydney, Gloucestershire GL15 6RG (01594 530272).

*Off route

Details of opening times should be checked with the *YHA Accommodation Guide* or with the hostels themselves.

TOURIST INFORMATION CENTRES

*Builth Wells: Groe Car Park, Builth Wells, Powys LD2 3BL (01982 553307).
Chepstow: Castle Car Park, Bridge Street, Chepstow, Gwent, NP6 5EY (01291 623772).
Hay-on-Wye: Oxford Road, Hay, Herefordshire HR3 5DG (01497 820144).
Hereford: 1 King Street, Hereford HR4 9BW (01432 268430).
Llandrindod Wells: Old Town Hall, Memorial Garden, Temple Street, Llandrindod Wells, Powys LD1 5DL (01597 822600).
*Monmouth: Shirehall, Agincourt Square, Monmouth, NP5 3DY (01600 713899).
*Rhayader: North Street, Rhayader, Powys LD6 5BU (01597 810591).
Ross-on-Wye: Swan House, Eddecross Street, Ross-on-Wye, Herefordshire HR9 7BZ (01989 562768).

*Seasonal opening only

USEFUL ADDRESSES

British Trust for Ornithology, Beech Grove, Tring, Hertfordshire HP1 5NR
CADW, Brunel House, 2 Fitzalan Road, Cardiff CF2 1UY (01222 500200).
Countryside Council for Wales, Plas Penrhos, Ffordd Penrhos, Bangor, Gwynedd LL57 2LQ (01248 370444).
English Heritage
Midlands: Hazelrigg House, 33 Marefair, Northampton NN1 1SR (01604 730320).
English Nature, Bronsil House, Eastnor, Near Ledbury, Herefordshire HR8 1EP (01531 638500).
National Trust
Severn: Mythe End House, Tewkesbury, Gloucestershire GL20 6EB (01684 850051).
South Wales: The King's Head, Bridge Street, Llandeilo, Dyfed SA19 6BB (01558 822800).
Ordnance Survey, Romsey Road, Maybush, Southampton, SO16 4GU.
Ramblers' Association, 1-5 Wandsworth Road, London SW8 2XX (0171 582 6878).
Royal Society for Nature Conservation, The Green, Witham Park, Waterside South, Lincoln LN5 7JR (01522 544400).
Royal Society for the Protection of Birds, The Lodge, Sandy, Bedfordshire SG19 2DL.

Wildlife Trusts

Gwent Wildlife Trust, 16 White Swan Court, Church Street, Monmouth, Gwent NP5 3BR.

Herefordshire Nature Trust, Community House, 25 Castle Street, Hereford HR1 2NW.

The Welsh Wildlife Trust, Upper Hurdley, Church Stoke, Powys SW15 6DY.

Youth Hostels Association, Trevelyan House, 8 St Stephens Hill, St Albans, Herefordshire AL1 2DY (01727 55215).

The Wye Valley Walk is managed by three county councils:

Rhayader to Hay-on-Wye

Rights of Way and Countryside Section, Planning Department, Powys County Council, County Hall, Llandrindod Wells, Powys LD1 5LG.

Hay-on-Wye to the Biblins (4 miles (6.5 km) east of Monmouth) The Countryside Service, Queenswood Country Park, Dinmore Hill, Leominster, Hereford and Worcester HR6 0PY.

The Biblins to Chepstow

Planning and Economic Development Department, Gwent County Council, Cwmbran, Gwent NP44 2XF.

ORDNANCE SURVEY MAPS COVERING THE WYE VALLEY WALK

Landranger Maps

(1: 50 000)

147	Elan Valley and Builth Wells
148	Presteigne and Hay-on-Wye
149	Hereford, Leominster
161	Abergavenny and the Black Mountains
162	Gloucester and Forest of Dean

Pathfinder Maps

(1: 25 0000)

969	Rhayader	1017	Hereford North
970	Llandrindod Wells	1040	Hereford South
992	Builth Wells	1041	Ledbury
1015	Aberedw	1065	Ross-on-Wye East
1038	Talgarth	1064	Ross-on-Wye West
1016	Hay-on-Wye		

Outdoor Leisure Maps (1: 25 000) No 14 (Wye Valley and the Forest of Dean) and No 13 (Brecon Beacons National Park – Eastern area)

BIBLIOGRAPHY

Cross, A. G. R., *Old Industrial Sites in Wyedean*, Cross, 1982
Dreghorn, W., *Geology Explained in the Forest of Dean and the Wye Valley*, David & Charles, 1968
Fletcher, H. L. V., *Portrait of the Wye Valley*, Robert Hale, 1968
Gibbings, Robert, *Coming Down the Wye*, Dent, 1943
Gilpin, Rev. William, *Observations on the River Wye*, 1770
Godwin, Fay & Toulson, Shirley, *The Drover's Roads of Wales*, Wildwood House, 1977
Grice, Frederick, *Kilvert's World*, Caliban Books, 1983
Helme, Andrew, *Monmouth and the River Wye*, Alan Sutton, 1989
Kilvert, Francis, *Selections from the Diary of the Rev. Francis Kilvert*, edited by William Plomer, Jonathan Cape, 1938-40
Kissack, Keith, *The River Wye*, Terence Dalton, 1978
Kissack, Keith, *Monmouth: The Making of a Country Town*, Phillimore, 1975
Knight, Jeremy K., *Chepstow Castle*, CADW, 1986
Lockwood, David, *Francis Kilvert*, Seren Books, 1990
Mason, Edmund J., *The Wye Valley From River Mouth to Hereford*, Robert Hale, 1987
Morris, M. M. *The Book of Ross-on-Wye*, Barracuda Books, 1980
Robinson, David M., *Tintern Abbey*, CADW, 1995
Taylor, A. J., *Monmouth Castle and Great Castle Museum*, HMSO, 1976
Wren, Derek, *Goodrich Castle*, English Heritage, 1993
—, *The Wye Valley*, Ward Lock, 1959

PLACES TO VISIT ON OR NEAR THE WYE VALLEY WALK

Rhayader Museum, East Street
* Elan Valley Visitor Centre
Builth Castle (CADW)
* Kilvert's Gallery, Clyro
Hay Castle (CADW), Hay-on-Wye
* Clifford Castle
* Arthur's Stone (chambered long barrow), Dorstone
Brobury House Gallery and Garden, Brobury
L'Escargot Anglais (National Snail Farming Centre), Credenhill
* The Weir Garden, Swainshill (NT)
Breinton Springs (NT)
Hereford: Herefordshire Waterworks Museum, Broomy Hill

City Museum and Art Gallery, Broad Street
Cathedral and chained library
Churchill Gardens Museum, Venn's Lane
Cider Museum and King Offa Distillery, Pomona Place
(off WhitecrossRoad)
The Old House, High Town
St John Medieval Museum, Coningsby Hospital,
Widemarsh Street

How Caple Court Gardens, How Caple

Ross-on-Wye: The Lost Street Museum, Palma Court, 27 Brookend
Street
The Button Museum, Kyrle Street

* Goodrich Castle (EH)
* Wye Valley Farm Park, Huntsham Court
* Jubilee Maze and Jubilee Park, Symonds Yat West

Monmouth: Nelson Collection and Local History Centre, Priory
Street
Castle and Great Castle House (CADW)
Monnow Bridge
Slaughterhouses

* Naval Temple and Round House, The Kymin (NT)

Tintern: Tintern Abbey (CADW)
Tintern Old Station

Chepstow: Chepstow Museum, Bridge Street
Chepstow Castle (CADW)

CADW = Welsh Historic Monuments
EH = English Heritage
NT = National Trust

* Off route